mcneff

From Your Friends At **The MAILBOX**®

MARCH

A MONTH OF REPRODUCIBLES AT YOUR FINGERTIPS!

D1364872

Grade 1

Editor:
Susan Hohbach Walker

Writers:
Catherine Broome, Amy Erickson, Sharon Murphy,
Susan Hohbach Walker, Kimberly Wombough

Art Coordinator:
Clevell Harris

Artists:
Cathy Spangler Bruce, Nick Greenwood, Clevell Harris,
Sheila Krill, Mary Lester, Rob Mayworth,
Kimberly Richard, Donna K. Teal

Cover Artist:
Jennifer Tipton Bennett

www.themailbox.com

©1998 by THE EDUCATION CENTER, INC.
All rights reserved.
ISBN #1-56234-223-1

Except as provided for herein, no part of this publication may be reproduced or transmitted in any form or by any means, electronic or mechanical, including photocopying, recording, or storing in any information storage and retrieval system or electronic online bulletin board, without prior written permission from The Education Center, Inc. Permission is given to the original purchaser to reproduce patterns and reproducibles for individual classroom use only and not for resale or distribution. Reproduction for an entire school or school system is prohibited. Please direct written inquiries to The Education Center, Inc., P.O. Box 9753, Greensboro, NC 27429-0753. The Education Center®, The Mailbox®, and the mailbox/post/grass logo are registered trademarks of The Education Center, Inc. All other brand or product names are trademarks or registered trademarks of their respective companies.

Manufactured in the United States

10 9 8 7 6 5 4 3

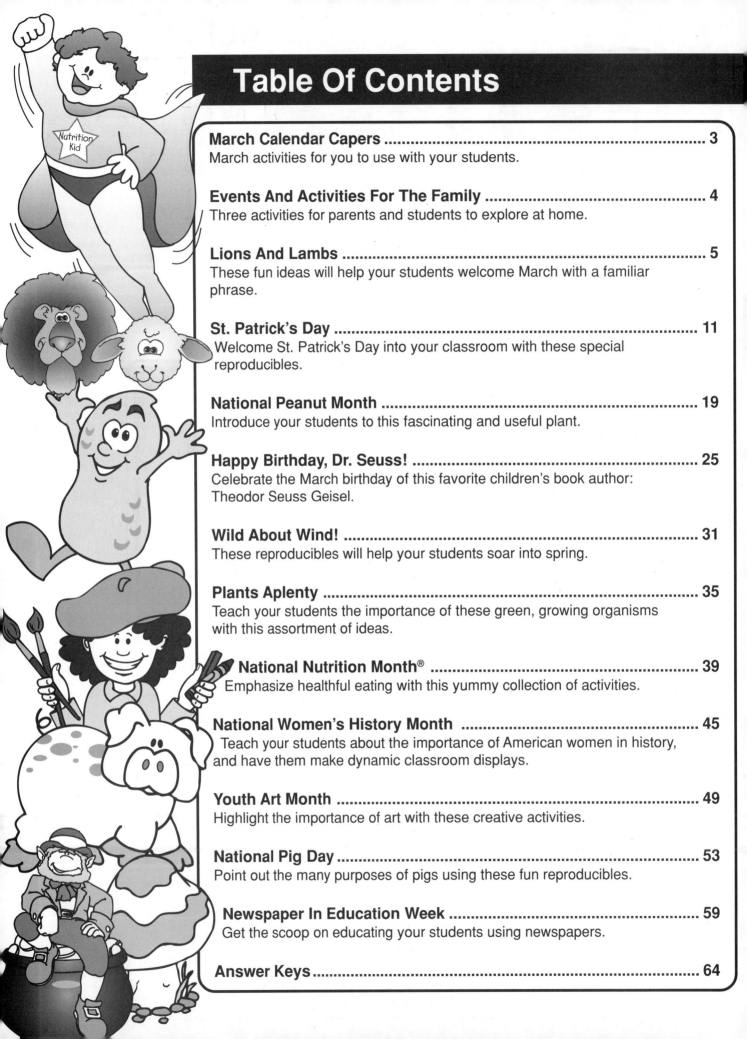

Table Of Contents

March Calendar Capers

Monday	Tuesday	Wednesday	Thursday	Friday
March 1 is Share A Smile Day. Discuss with students the saying "When you give away a smile, you receive one in return."	March 2 is the birthdate of Dr. Seuss. Celebrate his birthdate by reading aloud some of his well-known books, such as *The Cat In The Hat* and *Green Eggs And Ham*.	March 3 is I Want You To Be Happy Day. Ask each child to think of a person whom he would like to make happy, and encourage the youngster to do something nice for him or her.	March is National Peanut Month. Provide peanuts for students to sample. Then plant a few shelled peanuts in clear plastic cups and watch them sprout!	The first full week in March is National School Breakfast Week. Ask each child to plan a healthful breakfast for his family.
Ireland is often called the Emerald Isle because it's a land of beautiful green countryside. Have students look in a large box of crayons to find various shades of green.	The March observance of Youth Art Month recognizes the importance of art education for youngsters. Schedule a class field trip to an art museum or invite local artists to visit your class.	The Girl Scouts Of The USA was founded on March 12, 1912. Ask students to tell the class their favorite flavors of Girl Scout cookies. Then have students invent and name a new flavor!	March winds make it a great month to fly kites. Ask each youngster to draw a new design for a kite.	March 14 is Save A Spider Day. Have students brainstorm places that spiders could be found.
St. Patrick's Day is March 17. This holiday commemorates the patron saint of Ireland. Have each child imagine what it would be like if a holiday were named after him.	Enlist students' help in counting the number of students wearing green today. Make a class graph to show the results.	Straw Hat Week is celebrated each March about two weeks before Easter. Have each child draw and decorate a straw hat.	National Poison Prevention Week is the third week in March. Ask students to brainstorm household and school items that are poisonous.	Memory Day is celebrated on March 21. Have students list telephone numbers or addresses that would be helpful to memorize. Emergency 911 / Mom at work 656-7712 / Dad at work 338-7420
On March 25, 1775, George Washington planted pecan trees that were a gift from Thomas Jefferson. Provide a variety of nuts for students to sample; then have each child vote for his favorite.	Some people believe that four-leaf clovers bring good luck. Ask each child to describe an item that he thinks is lucky and explain why.	March 26 is Make Up Your Own Holiday Day. Have each student name this day for a holiday of his choice.	Coca-Cola® was invented on March 29, 1886. Invite students to sample several different beverages, including Coke®. Ask each child to identify the one that he likes best; then record the results on a class graph.	March is said to "come in like a lion and go out like a lamb." Ask students to tell what they think this expression means and whether or not it describes March's weather this year.

©1998 The Education Center, Inc. • *March Monthly Reproducibles* • Grade 1 • TEC944

3 **Note To The Teacher:** Highlight special days and events with these fact-filled ideas.

MARCH
Events And Activities For The Family

Directions: Select at least one activity below to complete as a family by the end of March. *(Challenge: See if your family can complete all three activities.)*

Lots Of Lions And Lambs

As the saying goes, "March comes in like a lion and goes out like a lamb." Discuss with your children the meaning of this expression. Then challenge them to solve this related problem: "If there are 12 legs, how many lions and lambs could there be?" Encourage youngsters to draw pictures or to use small items such as toothpicks to help them represent the legs and to solve the problem. Children may be surprised to discover that there is more than one solution. Help them determine all possible answers; then create additional problems for youngsters to try. What a "grr-eat" activity to reinforce problem-solving skills!

National School Breakfast Week

The first full week in March is dedicated to the importance of nutritious school breakfasts. Discuss with youngsters the importance of a healthful breakfast to start each day. Have them brainstorm nutritious breakfast foods; then enlist children's help in developing a breakfast menu for the week. Remind youngsters that the menu for each day should be balanced. Give each family member a role in preparing the meals, setting the table, and cleaning up afterward. Not only will children learn about good nutrition and responsibility, they'll have fun and develop a sense of pride in the process!

Memory Day

Don't forget to mark March 21 on your calendar! It's Memory Day! Engage your family in an entertaining oral memory game on this day. Begin the game by providing this story starter: "I'm going on a trip and I'm packing…" Then state one item to pack, such as a toothbrush or a sweater. The next family member repeats the story starter and your item, then adds one of his own. A player is "out" if he is unable to accurately remember all of the items in the correct sequence. Play continues in a similar fashion until only one person remains in the game. This person is then declared the winner. Now that's a memorable game!

©1998 The Education Center, Inc. • *March Monthly Reproducibles* • Grade 1 • TEC944

Note To The Teacher: Distribute one copy of this reproducible to each student at the beginning of the month. Encourage each family to complete at least one activity by the end of March.

LIONS AND LAMBS

"March comes in like a lion and goes out like a lamb!" Because this month falls between winter and spring, its days are often unpredictable. They may be blustery and harsh like a lion, or mild and gentle like a lamb. Treat your students to these fun activities to welcome March.

Chicken
Dog
Penguin
Dolphin
Deer
Whale
Frog
Cow
Lizard
Cougar
Mouse
Mon

Koala
Cat
Chicke
Rabb
Lio
S

Chicken
Penguin

Same	Different
Both are birds.	Penguin lives where it's cold. Chicken doesn't.
Both lay eggs.	Penguin can swim. Chicken can't swim.

Animal Comparisons

Comparing and contrasting the lion and the lamb will help your students learn about these animals and about similarities and differences. Continue this process by having your students compare and contrast other animals, too. First ask your students to brainstorm a list of animals. Have them select two; then write their names at the top of a chart as shown. Then have students begin listing ways that these animals are similar and different. Repeat this process as often as you'd like, using other animals from the original list.

Springtime Babies

The onset of spring is a wonderful time to teach your students about animals and their young. If possible contact a farm, a zoo, or an animal shelter and plan a trip to view young animals and their mothers. Back in the classroom, this fun activity will get students excited about animals' springtime babies. Write the name of an adult animal on a plain, white index card and its baby's name on another card. Repeat this process using different animals until you have a class supply of cards. Give a card to each child in the class and ask her to draw a picture of the animal. (Provide reference materials for students to look at.) When all the pictures are complete, have each child look for her partner by matching the adult animal to its baby.

Cow

Calf

Marching In

March

Sunday	Monday	Tuesday	Wednesday	Thursday	Friday	Saturday

Write in the dates for this month.
Write the answer to each question.

1. How many days are in this month?_____

2. How many Mondays are in this month? _____

3. On what day does the month begin?_____

4. What day is March 10 on? _____

5. What day is today? _____

6. What is the date on the second Thursday? _____

©1998 The Education Center, Inc. • *March Monthly Reproducibles* • Grade 1 • TEC944

Out On A Limb

Write the contraction for each pair of words.

Drop the **o**.

Add an **apostrophe**.

1.	does	not	*doesn't*
2.	is	not	_____
3.	was	not	_____
4.	have	not	_____
5.	did	not	_____
6.	were	not	_____
7.	do	not	_____
8.	has	not	_____
9.	could	not	_____
10.	would	not	_____

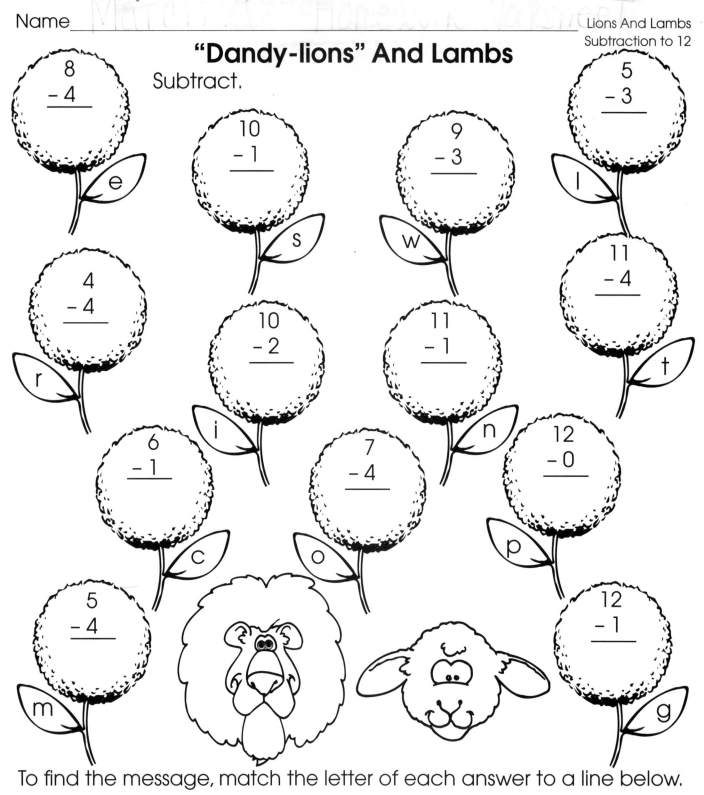

March 20th Homework Worksheet

Name_____

Lions And Lambs
Subtraction to 12

"Dandy-lions" And Lambs
Subtract.

To find the message, match the letter of each answer to a line below.

				,							
2	4	7	9		6	4	2	5	3	1	4

9	12	0	8	10	11

8   ©1998 The Education Center, Inc. • *March Monthly Reproducibles* • Grade 1 • TEC944 • Key p. 64

Loud And Quiet

When are you as loud as a lion,
or as quiet as a lamb?

Write.

_____

_____

_____

_____

_____

_____

_____

_____

_____

_____

_____

_____

_____

_____

_____

Lions And Lambs
Long vowels: *a, i, o, u*

The "Mane" Event

Name each picture.
Cut and glue each picture beside its matching vowel.

mane	ā			
five	ī			
bone	ō			
cube	ū			

©1998 The Education Center, Inc. • *March Monthly Reproducibles* • Grade 1 • TEC944

St. Patrick's Day

Long ago, the Irish set aside March 17 to honor Saint Patrick, the priest who brought Christianity to Ireland. The day commemorates his death in the year 461. It became a custom to wear a sprig of shamrock on this day because legend states that Saint Patrick used this three-leaf clover to explain the meaning of the Holy Trinity to his people. Today many people wear or display shamrocks on St. Patrick's Day.

Top Of The Morning To Ya!
Start your St. Patrick's Day celebration with a tasty breakfast! Serve up bowls of Lucky Charms® cereal and green milk (just add a few drops of green food coloring) for this morning feast. This tasty treat will have those Irish eyes a-smilin'!

So Lucky!
Ever wonder how some people seem to have all the luck? Well, a few might attribute it to good-luck charms. Show your students a four-leaf shamrock or clover (use a paper cutout if a real one is not available). Explain that because each stem of this plant usually has three leaves, finding one with four leaves is considered good luck. Have your students brainstorm other things that are considered to bring good luck; then have each child write about a good-luck charm that he has or would like to find. Encourage him to write how his good-luck charm brings him good luck. Display the finished writings on a bulletin board surrounded by four-leaf-clover cutouts. Good luck!

Name _____

Pot O' Coins

Count the coins.
Write the amount for each pot.
Color the pot with the greatest amount of gold.

©1998 The Education Center, Inc. • *March Monthly Reproducibles* • Grade 1 • TEC944 • Key p. 64

Name _____

Shamrock Clocks

Write the time below each
clock.

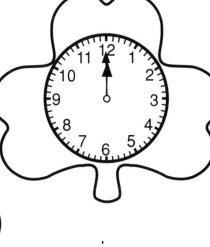

____ : ____ ____

____ : ____ ____

____ : ____ ____

____ : ____ ____

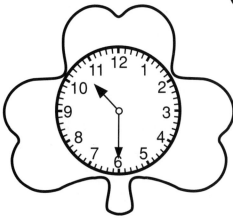

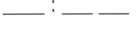

Bonus Box:
It's 4:00 now.
What time will it
be in two hours?

____ : ____ ____

____ : ____ ____

____ : ____ ____

Name _____

Leprechaun Land

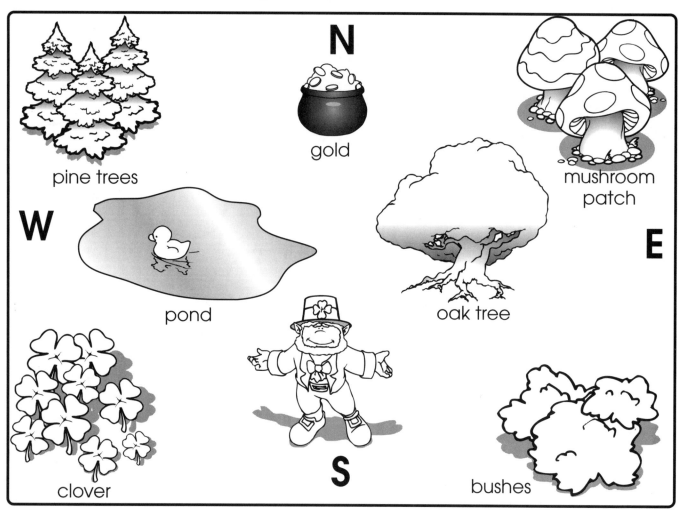

N

gold

pine trees

W

pond

mushroom patch

E

oak tree

clover

S

bushes

Read. Circle each answer. Write.

1. This is a map of a _____.

   person   place   thing

2. The pond is _____ of the oak tree.

   north   south   west

3. The pot of gold is _____ of the leprechaun.

   north   west   east

4. There are _____ pine trees.

   4   3   2

Bonus Box:
On the back of this sheet, draw a map of an imaginary place. Ask a friend questions about your map.

©1998 The Education Center, Inc. • *March Monthly Reproducibles* • Grade 1 • TEC944

Name _____

Lucky Day

Add or subtract.

Lucky Sam had 10 coins. He found 5 more. How many coins does Sam have now? _____ coins	There were 15 shamrocks. Jake took 4. How many shamrocks are left? _____ shamrocks

There were 13 mushrooms.
A rabbit ate 3.
How many mushrooms are
   left?
 	
_____ mushrooms
	There were 9 potatoes in the
	   pot.
	3 were taken out.
	How many potatoes are left?
	
	_____ potatoes

Erin saw 6 leprechauns.
Kelly saw 7 leprechauns.
How many leprechauns did
   they both see?
 	
_____ leprechauns
	Megan bought 8 lucky
	   charms.
	Her dad gave her 2.
	How many charms does she
	   have now?
	
	_____ charms

Write the number sentence.

Patrick saw 3 pots of gold.
He saw 10 more.
How many pots of gold did he see?

_____ : ____ ____

Name _____

Irish Jig

Write the blends.

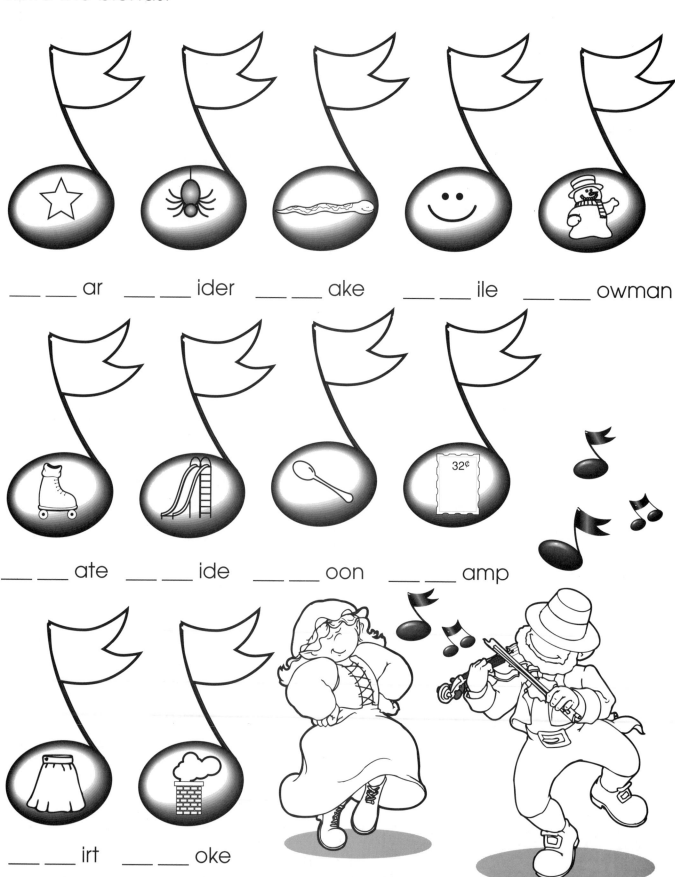

__ __ ar   __ __ ider   __ __ ake   __ __ ile   __ __ owman

__ __ ate   __ __ ide   __ __ oon   __ __ amp

__ __ irt   __ __ oke

©1998 The Education Center, Inc. • *March Monthly Reproducibles* • Grade 1 • TEC944

Name _____

Go For The Gold

Cut out the coins.
Use the coins to measure each object.

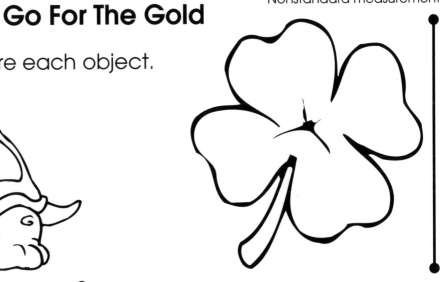

_____ coins

_____ coins

_____ coins

_____ coins

_____ coins

_____ coins

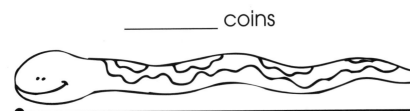

_____ coins

©1998 The Education Center, Inc. • *March Monthly Reproducibles* • Grade 1 • TEC944

Name _____

Mighty Mushroom

Write **sh, th, ch,** or **wh.**
Color by the code.

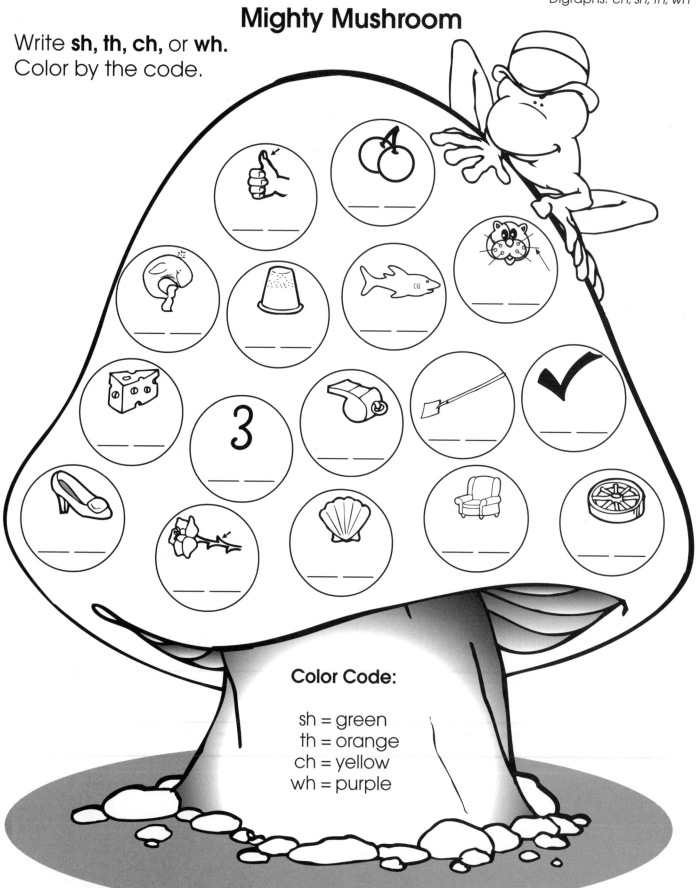

Color Code:

sh = green
th = orange
ch = yellow
wh = purple

Bonus Box: On the back of this sheet, draw two pictures that *end* with **sh** and **ch.**

©1998 The Education Center, Inc. • *March Monthly Reproducibles* • Grade 1 • TEC944

NATIONAL PEANUT MONTH

In search of a nutritious snack? Try some tasty peanuts! There's no better time than the present, since the month of March is National Peanut Month. This unit will help your students practice some basic skills while highlighting this nutty celebration.

Partner Peanut Paragraphs

Your students will be like two peanuts in a pod when they try this unique partner writing activity. Distribute a copy of page 23 to each child and ask her to write a story starter on the first set of lines. Encourage your students to use their imaginations to create far-fetched, outrageous, or hilarious introductions. If desired, ask each child to use a peanut theme. Next, pair students and ask each child to exchange her paper with her partner. Have each child read the story starter that her partner wrote. Based on that introduction, encourage each child to finish her partner's story and sign her own name on the last line. When the writing is complete, have partners exchange papers again and read the stories. Post these partner paragraphs for all to enjoy.

Peanut Possibilities

Thanks to George Washington Carver's pioneering research, peanuts now have hundreds of uses. The following list points out some of the many items that might contain peanuts, peanut oil, or peanut shells. Share the list with your students. If possible, bring some of these packaged items and have students look for peanut products on the labels. Then have groups of students generate lists of other items they think might contain peanut products.

- ice cream
- bread
- salad dressing
- margarine
- soap
- face powder
- shaving cream
- shampoo
- paint
- livestock feed
- plastics
- wallboard
- abrasives

Nuts About Numbers

1 [PEANUTS] = 10 peanuts

Write how many tens and ones.
Write the number.

2	**3**
tens	ones

23

---

tens	ones

tens	ones

tens	ones

tens	ones

tens	ones

tens	ones

tens	ones

tens	ones

tens	ones

©1998 The Education Center, Inc. • *March Monthly Reproducibles* • Grade 1 • TEC944

Pairs Of Peanuts

Read each word on the left.
Draw a line to match its opposite.

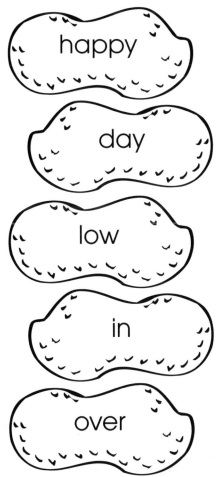

happy

day

low

in

over

night

high

sad

under

out

Read each sentence. Look at the bold word.
Think of a word that means the opposite.
Rewrite the sentence using that word.

1. This peanut tastes **bad.**

_____

_____

2. I like **soft** peanuts.

_____

_____

Bonus Box: On the back of this sheet, write two more pairs of opposites.

Cracked Up!

Find two words to make a compound word.
Write each compound word.
Color each shell after you use its word.

pine

rain

pop

door

base

paper

corn

cone

ball

news

bell

coat

1. _____

2. _____

3. _____

4. _____

5. _____

6. _____

 ©1998 The Education Center, Inc. • *March Monthly Reproducibles* • Grade 1 • TEC944

Name _____

Peanut Partners

Write.

_____

_____

_____

Exchange papers.
Write.

_____

_____

_____

_____

_____

_____

_____

_____

Story written by _____

©1998 The Education Center, Inc. • *March Monthly Reproducibles* • Grade 1 • TEC944

Note To The Teacher: Use with "Partner Peanut Paragraphs" on page 19.

Name _____

Piles Of Peanuts

Add.

```
  2        3        4        2
  3        2        4        7
+ 5      + 8      + 4      + 6
```

```
  5        6        3        6
  2        7        8        5
+ 4      + 3      + 5      + 1
```

```
  4        5        5        3
  3        3        6        9
+ 8      + 3      + 5      + 2
```

Bonus Box: On the back of this sheet, solve this problem: Pat ate 3 peanuts, then he ate 9 more. How many peanuts did Pat eat?

©1998 The Education Center, Inc. • *March Monthly Reproducibles* • Grade 1 • TEC944 • Key p. 64

Happy Birthday, Dr. Seuss!

Theodor Seuss Geisel, the creator of such memorable characters as the Grinch, Lorax, Cat In The Hat, and Horton, was born March 2, 1904, in Springfield, Massachusetts. This popular author is well-known for writing children's books filled with nonsense words and unbelievable characters. Although they are presented in a seemingly lighthearted fashion, many of his books actually address serious real-life issues. *The Lorax*, for example, is about protecting the environment. Other books were written specifically for young children who are just starting to read. In fact Geisel wrote *The Cat In The Hat* to provide an alternative to the "Dick and Jane" beginning readers.

Geisel, who died in 1991, wrote many of his books under the pseudonym of Dr. Seuss. Seuss was his mother's maiden name. He added "Dr." to please his father and because he was studying for his doctorate when he decided to become a cartoonist. He also used the pen name Theo LeSieg (Geisel spelled backwards).

With the current and long-lasting popularity of his books, it's hard to believe that Geisel was not readily accepted into the publishing world. His high-school art teacher once told him that he would never succeed as an artist, and the first book that he wrote, *And To Think That I Saw It On Mulberry Street*, was turned down by 28 publishers before it was finally published. Geisel went on to write more than 40 children's books and he illustrated many of them.

Coin Concentration

This money memory game is a great way to top off a reading of *The Cat In The Hat* (Random House Books For Young Readers, 1966). After sharing this entertaining book with students, have each child color the hats on a copy of page 27. Instruct children to leave the price tags white. Then ask each student to cut along the broken lines to create game cards. Pair students and direct each twosome to play using only one card set at a time. To play, a child from each pair shuffles the cards and arranges them facedown on a playing surface. In turn, each child flips over two cards. If he turns over a hat and its matching coin combination, the student may keep the cards. If they don't match, the child turns them facedown again. The child with the most cards at the end of the game wins. Now that's a memorable way to reinforce money skills!

Hats Off

Hats off to Geisel's unique characters! These humorous characters were often the result of doodling or unusual circumstances. The lovable Horton, for example, was created when a breeze blew one of Geisel's elephant drawings onto a sketch of a tree. The absurd picture that resulted prompted Geisel to ask himself why an elephant would be in a tree. The answer—to hatch an egg, of course! It was not long before Geisel wrote *Horton Hatches The Egg* (Random House Books For Young Readers, 1966).

After enjoying a variety of Dr. Seuss books, engage your students in a discussion about their favorite Dr. Seuss characters. Then ask each youngster to complete a copy of page 28. To do so, he writes his name, his favorite character's name, and the corresponding book title in the spaces provided. The student also draws a picture of the character and explains why he likes him. Have youngsters cut out their completed hats and display them in your classroom. For added fun that is sure to spark students' imaginations, invite each youngster to create his own character. Mount students' completed artwork on a bulletin board for a one-of-a-kind display. Who knows? One of these characters might find his way into a book some day!

Outlandish Tales

What youngster doesn't like to embellish his stories? The boy in *And To Think That I Saw It On Mulberry Street* (Random House Books For Young Readers, 1997) is no exception. His dad warns that he needs to stop "turning minnows into whales," but the boy is intent on telling a story that can't be beat. Read aloud this inventive tale; then try this engaging small-group activity to reinforce students' use of descriptive phrases. Begin by saying, "On the way back from school, I saw…" and invite a youngster to complete the sentence. Then have another student repeat the sentence and add one of her own. Continue in a like manner until everyone has had a turn exaggerating the story. For an imaginative alternative to this oral activity, record each student's sentence on a separate sheet of paper and have him illustrate it. Then compile and bind the pages with a cover to make an amusing class book. No doubt this will be one story that no one can beat!

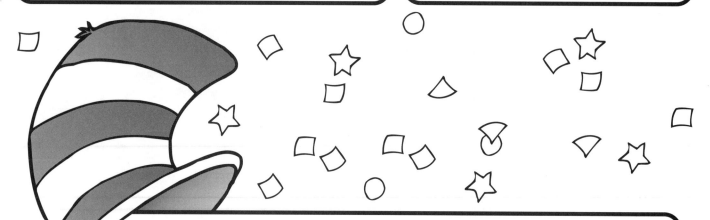

Delightful Dr. Seuss Books

These are just a few of the many titles that are sure to entertain your youngsters.
Daisy-Head Mayzie (Random House Books For Young Readers, 1995)
Fox In Socks (Random House Books For Young Readers, 1966)
If I Ran The Circus (Random House Books For Young Readers, 1966)
My Many Colored Days (Alfred A. Knopf, Inc.; 1996)
The Cat In The Hat Comes Back (Random House Books For Young Readers, 1966)
The Lorax (Random House Books For Young Readers, 1971)
There's A Wocket In My Pocket (Random House Books For Young Readers, 1974)
Wacky Wednesday by Theo. LeSieg (Beginner Books, 1974)

Coin Concentration

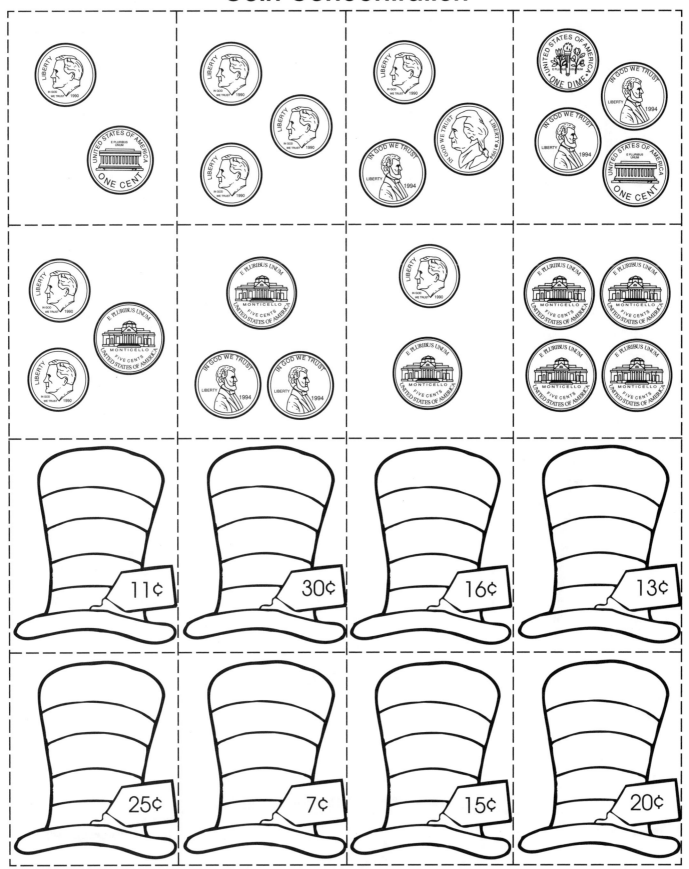

©1998 The Education Center, Inc. • *March Monthly Reproducibles* • Grade 1 • TEC944

Hats Off
To My Favorite Dr. Seuss Character

by _____

Character:

Title:

Picture:

Why I like this character:

©1998 The Education Center, Inc. • *March Monthly Reproducibles* • Grade 1 • TEC944

Note To The Teacher: Use with "Hats Off" on page 26.

Name _____

Rhyme Time

Cut. Match the rhymes .Glue. Write.

nest	
block	
bee	
cone	
truck	

Bonus Box:
On the back of your paper, write a sentence with a pair of rhyming words.

©1998 The Education Center, Inc. • *March Monthly Reproducibles* • Grade 1 • TEC944

Name _____

It All Started When...

Listen to *The Lorax.*
Pick a word to end each sentence.
Color the ◯.
Write.

The Once-ler made a _____ .
◯ factory
◯ house

The factory made _____ .
◯ sun
◯ smog

The birds could not _____ .
◯ fly
◯ sing

The pond got _____ .
◯ clean
◯ dirty

The fish went _____ .
◯ away
◯ home

Bonus Box: Think about what the Once-ler did. Write a letter to him on the back of your paper.

©1998 The Education Center, Inc. • *March Monthly Reproducibles* • Grade 1 • TEC944

Wild About Wind!

Journey into the air with a study of wind and kites using the high-flyin' ideas in this unit. Your students will soar with excitement over this topic!

The "Write" Kite

Children love to tell stories and they'll especially enjoy writing them in this clever kite-shaped journal. Make a construction-paper copy of page 34 for each child. Have her cut out the kite shape along the heavy black outline. Give each child an 18-inch piece of yarn and three 6" x 2" scraps of colorful material. Use a hole puncher to make a hole on the • and have the child tie one end of her yarn through the hole. Help each child knot her fabric scraps around the yarn to create bows on the kite tail. Then give each child several pages of plain or lined writing paper. Help her stack the writing paper behind the kite-shaped cover and staple the paper in place near the top of the kite. Then have each child trim the paper to the shape of the cover. Give students a writing topic or have them select their own. Ask each child to write her topic on the lines provided on the cover; then have her write her name where indicated. Next ask each child to write an original story on the pages of the journal. Have her decorate her cover and illustrate her book as desired. For additional ways to use this journal cover, see "High-Flyin' Ideas" on this page.

High-Flyin' Ideas

Make the most of the kite-shaped journal cover on page 34 by trying these useful ideas. To alter the look of the journal cover, mask the lines with white paper and duplicate to create a plain kite pattern; then add one of the suggestions listed below before duplicating a class supply. Follow the directions in "The 'Write' Kite" on this page to create the kite and kite tail.

— Print the letters "MARCH" vertically along the left side of the kite. Have each child complete the acrostic with words that tell about the month.
— Add a spelling list or vocabulary list to the front. After making the kite, students can display it at home while they study the words.
— Have students apply small, colorful squares of tissue paper with a light coat of glue. Display the finished decorations around your classroom.
— After a study of wind, write quiz questions on the kite shape. After students complete the quiz, have them finish their projects and display them in a hallway.

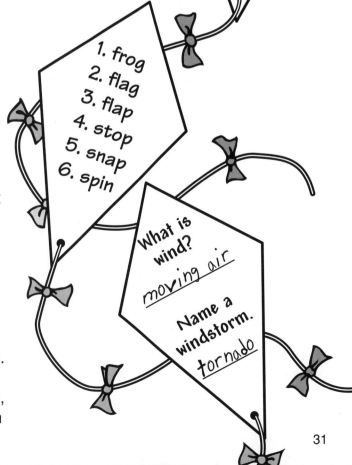

Wind Is...

Name _____

©1998 The Education Center, Inc.

flying hats! ①

bending trees! ②

sailing boats! ③

soaring kites! ④

Draw and write.

_____ ⑤

- -

Note To The Teacher: Have each child color the pages and cover and finish page 5. Then have the child cut on the heavy solid
lines, sequence the pages behind the cover, and staple in the left margin.

Flyin' Fractions

Read and color.

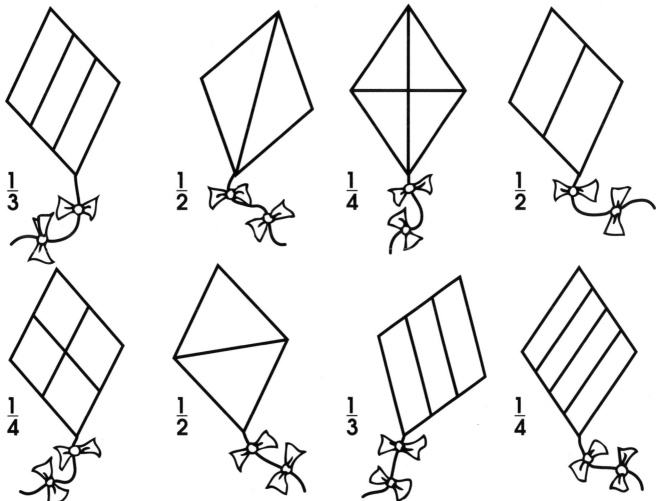

$\frac{1}{3}$ $\frac{1}{2}$ $\frac{1}{4}$ $\frac{1}{2}$

$\frac{1}{4}$ $\frac{1}{2}$ $\frac{1}{3}$ $\frac{1}{4}$

What fraction of each kite is colored?
Write.

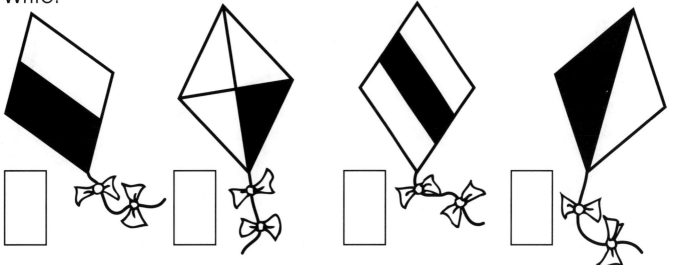

©1998 The Education Center, Inc. • *March Monthly Reproducibles* • Grade 1 • TEC944

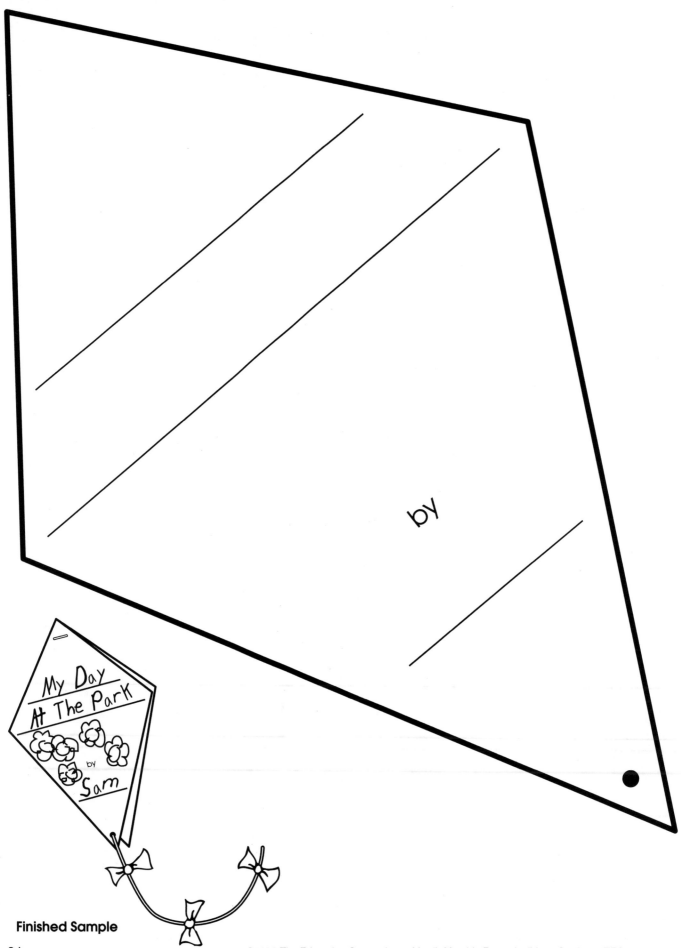

by

My Day
At The Park

by
Sam

Finished Sample

©1998 The Education Center, Inc. • *March Monthly Reproducibles* • Grade 1 • TEC944

PLANTS APLENTY

What's possibly the most common sign of spring? That's right! Green plants. You're sure to find plenty of helpful information in this unit to present the power of plants to your students.

Planting An Alphabet

Want a great way to organize your study of plants? While introducing your plant unit, challenge your students to find a plant-related word to match each letter of the alphabet. Throughout the study have your students be on the lookout for words that can complete the challenge. Each time a word is found, write it on a sheet of construction paper and ask a student to illustrate it, or have students cut pictures from magazines or seed catalogs. Display the finished posters in alphabetical order. By the time your plant study is finished, you'll have a terrific visual review right on your classroom wall!

This is a tulip. It is red. I saw it near the post office.

Picture Springtime!

Help your students picture springtime with this photographic activity. Prepare by bringing a Polaroid® camera and some film for this project. (If that's not available, plan time to develop your film.) On a pleasant spring day, take your students on a walk and ask each child to pick out a plant that he wants to photograph, such as a dandelion, grass, a blooming flower, or a tree. Give each child the opportunity to photograph his selected plant. If you're using film that needs to be developed, be sure to record the plant or photo number as each student takes his picture. To complete the project, give each child his developed picture and have him glue it to a sheet of construction paper. Then have him write a description of his plant on a lined index card and glue it below his plant's photo. Display the finished projects to bring a little spring into your school.

Potted Plants

Write the missing addend for each problem.
Use the flower.

Note To The Teacher: For help in solving, have each child color the number of flower petals to match the given addend. The remaining petals will reveal the missing addend.

36

Name_____

Picking Pansies

Read each sentence.
Write the long-vowel word.

_____

1. Can Ann plant seeds? _____

2. This flower is green. _____

3. Can Bill eat corn? _____

4. This plant has a big leaf. _____

5. Sam dug a hole for the bulb. _____

6. Is this a rose? _____

7. Did Ken make this salad? _____

8. Kim gave water to the plant. _____

9. This plant is huge! _____

10. Sid and Tom like to garden. _____

Name _____

38

Planting Plan

Cut and glue in order.

1	2	3	4	5

©1998 The Education Center, Inc. • *March Monthly Reproducibles* • Grade 1 • TEC944

Put in the seeds.

Watch the plant grow.

Dig a hole.

Cover the seeds with dirt.

Add water.

NATIONAL NUTRITION MONTH ®

Eating healthful foods is a key to staying healthy. During National Nutrition Month, teach your students about good nutrition and healthful eating habits. Serve up these nutritious ideas to get your unit started.

Daily Food Diary

Explain the categories of the Food Guide Pyramid to your students (see page 42). Ask them to name some of the foods they've eaten in the past day. Help them determine where on the Pyramid those foods would fit. After discussing other healthful food choices, distribute a copy of page 42 to each child. Instruct each student to take the paper home and record the foods he eats for one day. Then have each child bring his completed page back to school to complete the activity. Ask each child to circle all bread group items on his list with a yellow crayon. If he has at least six items circled, have him color the breads section of the pyramid yellow. Repeat the activity for each of the remaining food categories, using the chart on this page to determine the color and minimum suggested servings. Because fats, oils, and sweets are not recommended, a student should only color that section of his triangle if he has *not* eaten foods from that category.

Category	Color	Minimum Amount
Breads	Yellow	6
Vegetables	Green	3
Fruit	Red	2
Milk	Blue	2
Meat	Orange	2
Fats, Oils, Sweets	Black	Use Sparingly

Name _____

The Price Is Right!

~Menu~

milk .... 3¢
juice .... 2¢
water .... 0¢

salad .... 5¢
apple .... 4¢
orange .... 4¢

bread .... 3¢
rice .... 6¢

chicken .... 8¢
fish .... 9¢
hamburger .... 7¢
hot dog .... 6¢
carrots .... 4¢
peas............................. 5¢
green beans .... 6¢
pudding .... 5¢

Write each amount. Use the menu.
Add to find the cost of each order.

milk _____¢ chicken _____¢ rice _____¢ [____]¢	fish _____¢ carrots _____¢ pudding _____¢ [____]¢	peas _____¢ hot dog _____¢ apple _____¢ [____]¢
salad _____¢ rice _____¢ water _____¢ [____]¢	orange _____¢ hamburger _____¢ green beans _____¢ [____]¢	fish _____¢ rice _____¢ bread _____¢ [____]¢

Bonus Box: On the back of this sheet, list the 3 foods you would order. Add to find the cost.

©1998 The Education Center, Inc. • March Monthly Reproducibles • Grade 1 • TEC944

Finding The Facts

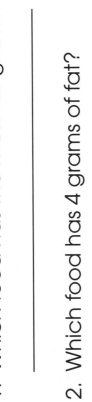

Food (1 serving)	Fat Grams
strawberries	0
milk (1%)	3
chicken (skinless)	3
beef hot dog	13
peas	0
white rice	1
frozen yogurt	4
french fries	12
baked potato	0
chicken nuggets	9
chocolate donut	21
toaster tart	5

Answer each question. Use the chart.

1. Which food has the most fat grams?

   _____

2. Which food has 4 grams of fat?

   _____

3. How many grams of fat are in peas?

   _____ grams

4. You eat a beef hot dog and peas. How many grams
   of fat do you eat? _____ grams

5. Which foods have the fewest fat grams?

   _____

6. How many more fat grams are in a toaster tart than
   in frozen yogurt? _____ gram

©1998 The Education Center, Inc. • *March Monthly Reproducibles* • Grade 1 • TEC944

Name_____

Daily Diet

Write each food you eat today.

_____

_____

_____

_____

_____

_____

Color as directed.

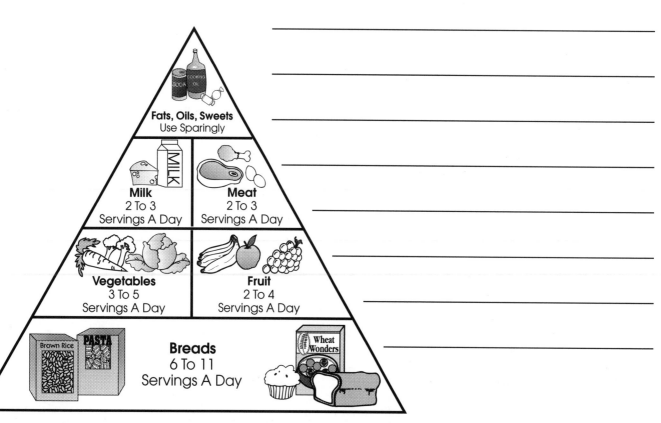

_____

_____

_____

_____

_____

_____

©1998 The Education Center, Inc. • *March Monthly Reproducibles* • Grade 1 • TEC944

Note To The Teacher: Use with "Daily Food Diary" on page 39.

Food Fun

Listen and do.

Finished Example

**Fats,
Oils, Sweets**
Use sparingly.

SODA

COOKING
OIL

Milk
2-3 daily servings

MILK

Meat
2-3 daily servings

Vegetables
3-5 daily servings

©1998 The Education Center, Inc. • *March Monthly Reproducibles* • Grade 1 • TEC944

Note To The Teacher: Duplicate pages 43 and 44 on white construction paper. Have each child cut out the pieces and glue together the two halves of the Bread category. Ask each child to cut pictures of food from magazines and glue them to the appropriate piece (front or back). Help each child punch holes and assemble the mobile with string as shown.

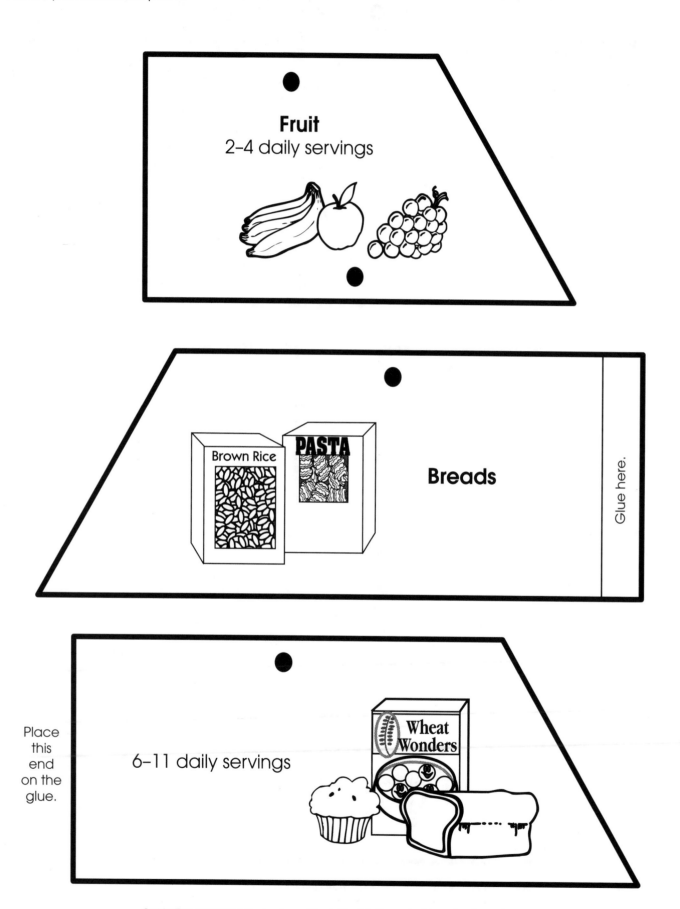

Fruit
2–4 daily servings

Brown Rice

PASTA

Breads

Glue here.

6–11 daily servings

Wheat Wonders

Place
this
end
on the
glue.

©1998 The Education Center, Inc. • *March Monthly Reproducibles* • Grade 1 • TEC944

Note To The Teacher: Duplicate on white construction paper. See the directions on page 43.

National WOMEN'S HISTORY Month

March has been named National Women's History Month. Participate with these star-studded activities honoring the women who have inspired our country from sea to shining sea.

Historic Women

Teach your students about an array of fascinating American women; then have them complete this project to display what they have learned. In advance, research some or all of the women listed below (or recognize others who are not listed). You may especially want to focus on those indicated with "*" since their portraits can be found on page 48. After presenting the information to your students, ask each child to select one of the women to feature in his project. Using the directions on this page, have each child complete a stand-up display.

- Marian Anderson*—She was the first Black woman to sing at the Metropolitan Opera.
- Amelia Earhart*—She was the first woman to fly a solo flight across the Atlantic Ocean.
- Hellen Keller*—Deaf and blind herself, she worked to help others who were deaf and blind.
- Wilma Mankiller—She was the first woman to become the chief of the Cherokee Nation.
- Barbara McClintock—She won the Nobel Prize in physiology for her research in genetics.
- Eleanor Roosevelt*—While redefining the role of First Lady, she defended the rights of minorities, women, and the poor.

How To Make A Stand-Up Display

1. Photocopy pages 46 and 47 for each child.
2. Have each student cut along the heavy solid outlines; then have him glue the panels together as shown.
3. Make several copies of page 48 and give each student a copy of one portrait—the woman he selected to feature on his display. (If a student chooses to feature a woman whose picture is not on page 48, photocopy and trim her picture to fit in the blank oval.)
4. Have each child cut out the picture and glue it to the oval on the left panel of his display. Ask him to write his name where indicated.
5. On the right panel, have each child write the name of the woman he featured; then have him write a brief comment about her achievements.

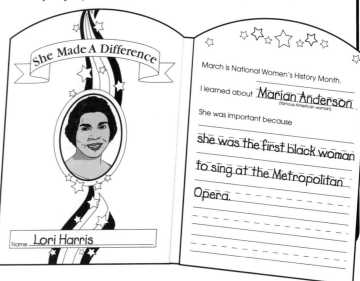

She Made A Difference

Name _____

©1998 The Education Center, Inc. • *March Monthly Reproducibles* • Grade 1 • TEC944

Note To The Teacher: Use with "Historic Women" on page 45.

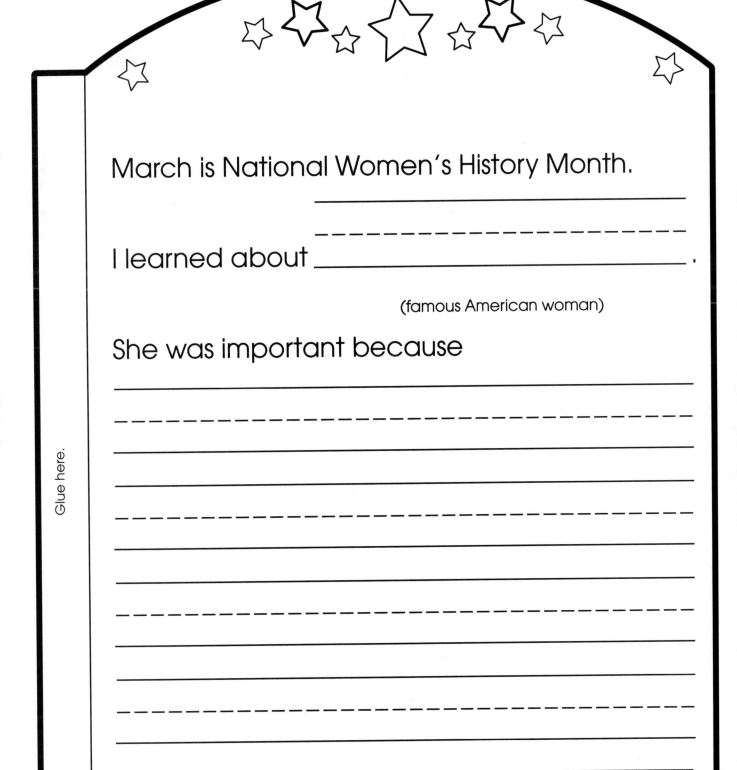

March is National Women's History Month.

_____

I learned about _____.

(famous American woman)

She was important because

_____

_____

_____

_____

_____

_____

_____

_____

_____

_____

Glue here.

©1998 The Education Center, Inc. • *March Monthly Reproducibles* • Grade 1 • TEC944

Note To The Teacher: Use with "Historic Women" on page 45.

Marian Anderson

Hellen Keller

Amelia Earhart

Eleanor Roosevelt

©1998 The Education Center, Inc. • *March Monthly Reproducibles* • Grade 1 • TEC944

Note To The Teacher: Use with "Historic Women" on page 45.

YOUTH ART MONTH

Encourage your students to express themselves through art during Youth Art Month—celebrated annually in March. The creative projects on these reproducibles will help you introduce your students to the wonderful world of creativity.

SHAPE ART

No two projects will look alike when you display the results of this unique activity. Give each child a four-inch square of construction paper or poster board. Ask him to cut the square into any shape he desires. Distribute a 9" x 12" sheet of white construction paper to each child and instruct him to trace his precut shape onto the paper several times, overlapping lines in some cases. Then have him use different colors to paint or color each of the sections. Display these one-of-a-kind projects to add a colorful touch to your classroom.

Kim

NAME THAT PICTURE

What's more personal than art that reflects your own name? Each child will love this personalized art project that uses the first letter of her first or last name. Give each child a copy of page 50. Ask her to draw her initial anywhere inside the frame with a black crayon. Then have her rotate the paper a quarter turn and look at the letter from a new perspective. Ask her to imagine the letter as part of a bigger picture. Have her continue to turn the paper and look at the letter until deciding on the best angle for creating a picture. Have each child draw the picture incorporating the letter that's already on the page, then color. Before displaying the project, ask each child to write her name on the frame above her picture.

©1998 The Education Center, Inc. • *March Monthly Reproducibles* • Grade 1 • TEC944

Note To The Teacher: Use with "Name That Picture" on page 49.

Name _____

Art Smart

Write the name of each art tool. Use the word box.

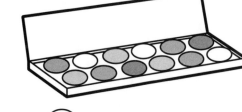

1.  ○

2. _____ ○

3. _____ ○

4. _____ ○

Word Box
paper
glue
scissors
paints
brushes

5. _____ ○

What tool is holding this artist's paper?

Write each circled letter to find the answer.

○ ○ ○ ○ ○

Bonus Box: What is your favorite art tool?
Write about using it on the back of this sheet.

Name _____

Color Combinations

Color or paint.

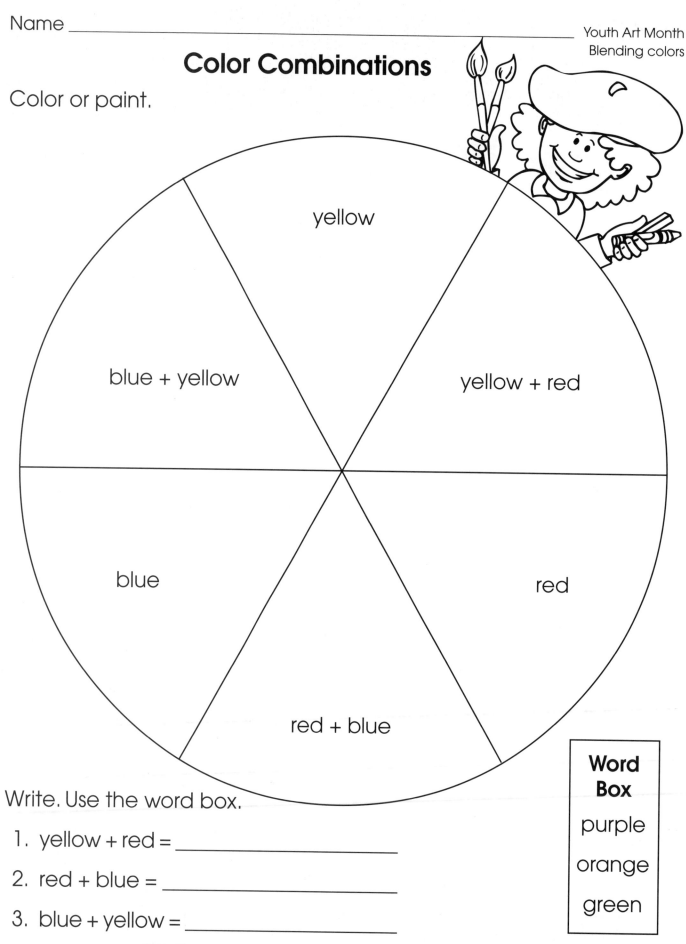

yellow

blue + yellow

yellow + red

blue

red

red + blue

Word Box

purple

orange

green

Write. Use the word box.

1. yellow + red = _____

2. red + blue = _____

3. blue + yellow = _____

©1998 The Education Center, Inc. • *March Monthly Reproducibles* • Grade 1 • TEC944

Note To The Teacher: Before using this sheet, have students experiment with mixing colors. Have them use paints or colored transparency film to blend colors.

NATIONAL PIG DAY

The pig, one of the most intelligent and useful domesticated animals, is recognized annually on March 1. Many people mistakenly assume that pigs are dirty because they roll in mud. While it's true that pigs wallow in mud, it's surprising to note that they are actually cleaner than most farm animals. Pigs roll in mud to keep cool because they have no sweat glands. Poor eyesight forces these barnyard animals to depend on a keen sense of smell to find food, such as corn and grains. Pigs provide approximately one-fourth of the meat eaten in the United States, including pork chops, ham, bacon, sausage, bologna, and salami. Pigs are also a valuable source of many other items, such as lard, leather, brushes, and medicines.

Tales With A Twist

Students will go hog-wild over this "Three Little Pigs" activity! First prepare a story-comparison chart like the one shown. Then read aloud a traditional retelling of this story, such as *The Three Little Pigs* by Margot Zemach (Farrar, Straus & Giroux, Inc.; 1997). Record the story information on the chart with students' help. Then gather a few other versions of this tale. Unique selections include *The Three Little Wolves And The Big Bad Pig* by Eugene Trivizas (Simon & Schuster Children's Division, 1997) and *The True Story Of The Three Little Pigs!* by A. Wolf as told to Jon Scieszka (Puffin Books, 1996). After sharing each story with students, invite them to help you add the titles and relevant information to the chart. Use the completed chart to compare and contrast the books with students. Then have your young authors write their own creative versions of "The Three Little Pigs." What a great way to boost students' critical-thinking skills and spark their imaginations at the same time!

Title	Characters	Problem	Solution
The Three Little Pigs	Momma 3 pigs wolf man	The wolf blew down the pigs' houses.	The third pig tricked the wolf.
The Three Little Wolves And The Big Bad Pig	3 wolves Mother kangaroo pig flamingo	The pig destroyed the wolves' houses.	The pig decided to be friends with the wolves.
The True Story Of The 3 Little Pigs!	wolf 3 pigs police news reporters	The wolf needed a cup of sugar. He bothered the pigs when he asked to borrow some.	The wolf went to jail.

Penny-Wise Students

Bank on this valuable idea to motivate students! Decorate a small glass jar with a pig cutout or obtain a piggy bank. Determine one or two student behaviors that you'd like to reinforce, such as working quietly or finishing assignments on time. Drop a penny into the jar or piggy bank each time youngsters demonstrate the specified behaviors. Periodically help students count the pennies and exchange them for equivalent coins. After youngsters have earned a predetermined amount, cash in the coins for a class reward, such as an extra recess or a special game. No doubt good behavior will add up with this idea. Plus coin-counting skills will improve too!

Name _____

All About Pigs

Read the story.

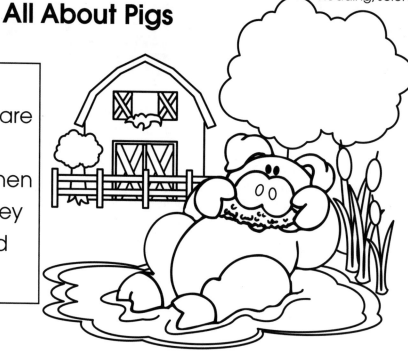

Pigs

Pigs live on farms. Pigs are clean animals. They are smart. Pigs roll in mud when it is hot. Pigs eat corn. They have small eyes. Pigs find food by smelling it.

Answer the questions.

1. Where do pigs live?

_____

_____

2. What do pigs do when it is hot?

_____

_____

3. How do pigs find food?

_____

_____

4. What do pigs eat?

_____

_____

Bonus Box: Imagine that pigs could talk. What would they say? Write a story on the back of this sheet.

 ©1998 The Education Center, Inc. • *March Monthly Reproducibles* • Grade 1 • TEC944

Farmyard Fun

Read each clue. Write the words. Use the word box.

1. not little

2. to make a hole

3. farm animal

4. a dance

5. small branch

6. a fruit

7. home for pigs

8. place to save money

Word Box

dig   twig

pig   big

fig   jig

pigpen   piggy bank

Bonus Box: Choose three *ig* words. On the back of this sheet, use each word in a sentence.

©1998 The Education Center, Inc. • *March Monthly Reproducibles* • Grade 1 • TEC944

Name _____

Piggy-Bank Puzzlers

Read the clues. Cut and glue each name below the matching pig.

Peter Pig has more than 25¢.

Peggy Pig has an even number of coins.

Pam Pig has a penny.

Read and solve.

1. Beth has 40¢ in her piggy bank. She adds 2 dimes. How much does she have now?

   [ ] ¢

2. Byron has 30¢. He spends 10¢. How much does he have now?

   [ ] ¢

©1998 The Education Center, Inc. • March Monthly Reproducibles • Grade 1 • TEC944

| Peter | Peggy | Pam |

Math Mystery

Subtract. Color a matching puzzle piece for each answer.

12 – 4 = _____   10 – 9 = _____   12 – 6 = _____

9 – 5 = _____   6 – 2 = _____   11 – 8 = _____

10 – 4 = _____   9 – 0 = _____   8 – 7 = _____

8 – 2 = _____   5 – 4 = _____   12 – 9 = _____

10 – 6 = _____   7 – 6 = _____   11 – 2 = _____

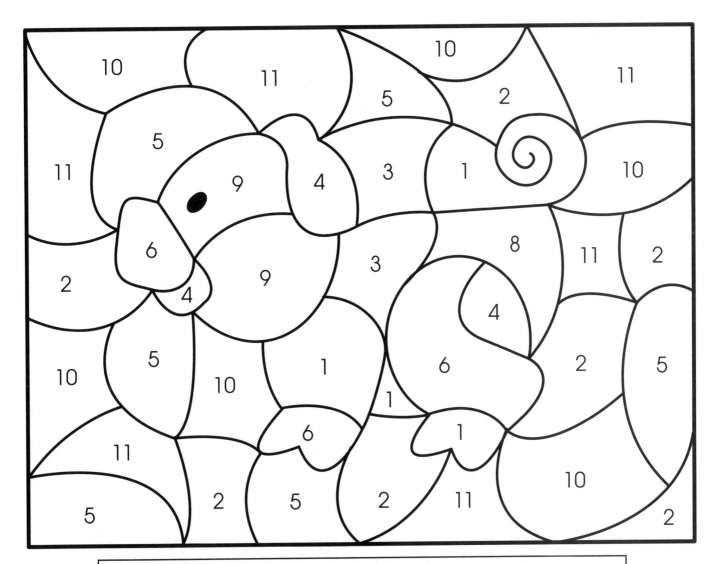

Bonus Box: On the back of this sheet, write a subtraction word problem about pigs.

Name _____

A Pig Tale

Rewrite each sentence. Put a **.** or a **?** at the end.

1. Who was in the pond

_____

_____

2. The ducks were in the pond

_____

_____

3. The pig was very hot

_____

_____

4. Did he go in the pond

_____

_____

5. The animals jumped in

_____

_____

6. Did they have fun

_____

_____

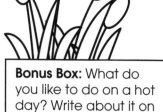

Bonus Box: What do you like to do on a hot day? Write about it on the back of this sheet.

©1998 The Education Center, Inc. • *March Monthly Reproducibles* • Grade 1 • TEC944

Note To The Teacher: To introduce the lesson, read aloud *The Pig In The Pond,* by Martin Waddell (Candlewick Press, 1996).

NEWSPAPER IN EDUCATION WEEK

Looking for an inexpensive and convenient educational resource? If so, look no further than your local newspaper! Not only is this publication ideal for a variety of language arts activities, it is perfect for math, social studies, and many other subjects as well. Feature this versatile educational resource during Newspaper In Education Week, annually the first full week in March. Now that's an idea that will really deliver!

Be On The Lookout!

This newsworthy search adds up to a lot of learning fun! Gather several newspapers and have each student cut out one short article. Give each youngster a copy of page 60 and review the words in the Word Box. Then instruct each child to look for the listed words in his article and mark each of them with the color indicated. Next ask each child to count how many times he found each word and have him write the number on the corresponding line in his Word Box. Instruct students to respond to the questions below the Word Box, then share their work and compare results. If desired help students create and analyze a class graph that shows the total number of times youngsters found each word. What a great way to give your young newspaper sleuths sight-word practice!

Hot Off The Press

Classroom events will be today's top story with this meaningful writing activity! Enlist students' help in publishing an edition of the "Class Tribune" (reproducible on page 63). To begin, ask youngsters to brainstorm recent and upcoming events, achievements, topics of study, and other noteworthy class news while you record their ideas on the chalkboard. Then, during small group shared-writing sessions, write short articles about some of these ideas on chart paper. After the articles have been finalized, copy them onto a photocopy of page 63. Add information in the "Help Wanted" department, such as volunteers or materials needed, or suggestions for parents to reinforce skills at home. Then duplicate a class supply of the completed newspaper. After reading it with students, have each youngster take a copy home to share with family members. Parents will enjoy reading about classroom happenings hot off the press and youngsters' language arts skills will be reinforced as well!

Be On The Lookout!

Listen and do.
Count. Write.

```
┌─────────────────────────────────────────────────┐
│                    Word Box                       │
│                                                   │
│   the _____ (yellow)      to _____ (orange)   │
│                                                   │
│   of _____ (blue)         in _____ (pink)     │
│                                                   │
│   and _____ (red)         is _____ (brown)    │
│                                                   │
│   a _____ (green)        you _____ (purple)   │
└─────────────────────────────────────────────────┘
```

Read each question.
Write the answer.

1. What word or words did you find the most times?

   _____
   _____

2. What word or words did you find the fewest times?

   _____
   _____

3. How many times in all did you find the words "the" and "of"?

   _____
   _____

4. How many times in all did you find the words "you" and "to"?

   _____

Bonus Box: On the back of this sheet, write the words in order from the word that you saw the fewest times to the word that you saw the most times.

©1998 The Education Center, Inc. • *March Monthly Reproducibles* • Grade 1 • TEC944

Now Showing...

Read. Cut.
Glue each time and movie title
  below the matching clock.

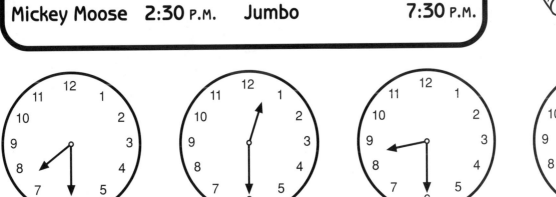

Super Cinema

Donald's Duck	8:30 P.M.	Wizard Of Laws	12:30 P.M.
Mickey Moose	2:30 P.M.	Jumbo	7:30 P.M.

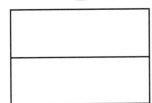 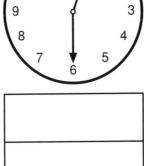 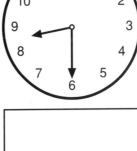 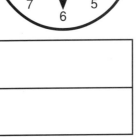 

Read each question. Write the answer.

1. What movie will be shown first?

    _____

    _____

2. What movie will be shown after Jumbo?

    _____

    _____

Bonus Box: What movie will be shown two hours after Wizard Of Laws? Draw a star beside it.

©1998 The Education Center, Inc. • *March Monthly Reproducibles* • Grade 1 • TEC944

8:30	2:30	12:30	7:30
Donald's Duck	Jumbo	Mickey Moose	Wizard Of Laws

Front-Page News

**Good newspaper stories tell
who, what, when, where, why, and how.**
Read the story. Answer the questions.

The Classroom Times

On Monday Miss Smith's class

sold candy at school to raise money.

All of the students worked

together. They will use the money

for a field trip.

1. **Who** sold candy?

   _____

   -

   _____

2. **When** did the class sell candy?

   _____

   -

3. **Where** did the class sell candy?

   _____

   -

Follow the directions.
   1. Draw a line under the sentence that tells **what** the class will do
      with the money.
   2. Circle the word that tells **how** the students worked.

Bonus Box: On the back of this sheet, tell **why** the class sold candy.

©1998 The Education Center, Inc. • *March Monthly Reproducibles* • Grade 1 • TEC944

Class Tribune

Teacher: **Date:**

Special Feature

Spotlight On...
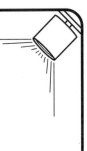

Upcoming Events

High-Flying Learning Fun

Help Wanted

©1998 The Education Center, Inc. • *March Monthly Reproducibles* • Grade 1 • TEC944

Note To The Teacher: Use with "Hot Off The Press" on page 59.

Answer Keys

Page 7

1. doesn't
2. isn't
3. wasn't
4. haven't
5. didn't
6. weren't
7. don't
8. hasn't
9. couldn't
10. wouldn't

Page 8

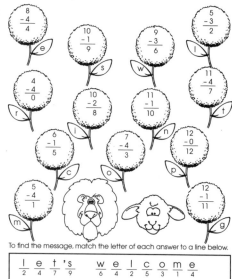

To find the message, match the letter of each answer to a line below.

l e t ' s   w e l c o m e
2 4 7 9   6 4 2 5 3 1 4

s p r i n g
9 12 0 8 10 11

Page 12

Page 24

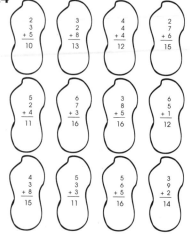

Page 36

Page 37

Read each sentence.
Write the long-vowel word.

1. Can Ann plant seeds? **seeds**
2. This flower is green. **green**
3. Can Bill eat corn? **eat**
4. This plant has a big leaf. **leaf**
5. Sam dug a hole for the bulb. **hole**
6. Is this a rose? **rose**
7. Did Ken make this salad? **make**
8. Kim gave water to the plant. **gave**
9. This plant is huge! **huge**
10. Sid and Tom like to garden. **like**

Page 51

1. b r u s h (e) s
2. p (a) i n t s
3. s c i (s) s o r s
4. p a p (e) r
5. g (l) u e

(e) (a) (s) (e) (l)

Page 57

12 - 4 = **8**   10 - 9 = **1**   12 - 6 = **6**
9 - 5 = **4**   6 - 2 = **4**   11 - 8 = **3**
10 - 4 = **6**   9 - 0 = **9**   8 - 7 = **1**
8 - 2 = **6**   5 - 4 = **1**   12 - 9 = **3**
10 - 6 = **4**   7 - 6 = **1**   11 - 2 = **9**

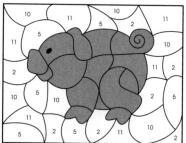